Cats IN BASKETS

Cats IN BASKETS

Kat Scratching

amber
BOOKS

Published by
Amber Books Ltd
74–77 White Lion Street
London
N1 9PF
United Kingdom
www.amberbooks.co.uk
Appstore: itunes.com/apps/amberbooksltd
Facebook: www.facebook.com/amberbooks
Twitter: @amberbooks

ISBN: 978-1-78274-545-7

Project Editor: Sarah Uttridge
Designer: Keren Harragan
Picture Research: Terry Forshaw

Printed in China

PICTURE CREDITS

Depositphotos: 10 (Kucher Serhii), 12 (The Kuzmins), 15 (Martin Kollar), 16 (Oksixx), 17 (Anmfoto), 18 (Volha Ahranovich), 19 (Africa-studio.com), 21 (Fotomt), 22 (Uzhursky), 23 (Africa-studio.com), 24 (Roman Pyshchyk), 25 (Vadim Borkin), 26 (Lufi Morgan), 27 (Mak80), 30 (Oksun70), 31 (Elena Elisseeva)

Dreamstime: 5 (Photodeti), 6 (Larisa Lafitskaya), 7 (Vvvita), 8 (Evgeniya Tiplyashina), 9 (Oleksandr Lytvynenko), 11 (Photowitch), 13 (Mnogosmyslov Aleksey) 14 (Vvvita), 20 (Angela Luchianuc), 28 (One Touch Spark), 29 (Maksimka3738), 32 (Hwongcc), 33 (Alexandr Vasilyev), 34 (Komar), 35 (Irina Khudolly), 36 (Irina Shoyhet), 37 (Vvvita), 38 (Max Wanted Media), 39 (Slubka), 40 (Vvvita), 41 (Alexey Poprotskiy), 42 (Ann Worthy), 43 (Robo123), 44 (Irina Khudolly), 45 (Brett Critchley), 46 (Anna Krivitskaia), 47 (Vvvita), 48 (Anna Krivitskaia), 49 (Zaretskaya), 50-51 (Altaoosthuizen), 52 (Countrymama), 53 (Fotomod), 54 (Fotograf77), 55 (Vvvita), 56 (Karen Anne Carnahan), 57 (Olga Volodina), 58 (Vvvita), 59 (Pixbull), 60 (Linn Currie), 61 (Mohamad Rizduan Abdul Rashid), 62 (Vvvita), 63 (Photodeti), 64 (Micuro), 65-66 (Vvvita), 67 (Gabe 9000c), 68 (Dmitry Dikushin), 69 (Pproman), 70 (Vvvita), 71 (Pproman), 72 (Miraswonderland), 73 (Sheila Fitzgerald), 74 (Gurinaleksandr), 75 (Okssi68), 76 (Sheila Fitzgerald), 77 (Indyammy), 78 (Vladimir Bryukhovetskiy), 79 (Alexey Savchuk), 80 (Tchara), 81 (Pandara), 82 (Jason Ondreicka), 83 (Virgonira), 84 (Tony Campbell), 85 (Bora Ucak), 86 (Alexey Savchuk), 87 (Ampack), 88 (Alexey Usachev), 89 (Molishka1988), 90 (Tony Campbell), 91 (Beijing Hetuchuangyi Images), 92 (Kucher Serhii), 93 (Vvvita), 94 (Vera Simon), 95 (Nataliya Lukhanina), 96 (Vvvita)

What could be cuter than a cat?

A cat in a basket.

In these pages, we present more than 90 photographs of the sweetest looking cats that you will ever see. Some are snuggled up, others are peeking out; some are playful kittens, others are sleepy old cats; some are stretching, others busy grooming; some solitary, others tumbling about with their brothers and sisters. But from being tucked up at home in a laundry basket to enjoying a day out in a picnic hamper, these cats and kittens are all undeniably very cute.